# HOW NOT TO GET EATEN

WRITTEN BY
## Josette Reeves

ILLUSTRATED BY
## Asia Orlando

**Author** Josette Reeves
**Illustrator** Asia Orlando
**Acquisitions Editor** James Mitchem
**Project Art Editor** Charlotte Milner
**Designer** Bettina Myklebust Stovne
**Design assistance** Holly Price, Sif Nørskov
**Production Editor** Abi Maxwell
**Senior Production Controller** Francesca Sturiale
**Publishing Coordinator** Issy Walsh
**Jacket Designer** Charlotte Milner
**Deputy Art Director** Mabel Chan
**Publishing Director** Sarah Larter

First published in Great Britain in 2022 by
Dorling Kindersley Limited
DK, One Embassy Gardens, 8 Viaduct Gardens,
London, SW11 7BW

The authorised representative in the EEA is
Dorling Kindersley Verlag GmbH. Arnulfstr. 124,
80636 Munich, Germany

A CIP catalogue record for this book
is available from the British Library.
ISBN: 978-0-2415-3845-6

Printed and bound in China

For the curious
www.dk.com

This book was made with Forest
Stewardship Council ™ certified
paper – one small step in DK's
commitment to a sustainable future.

For more information go to
www.dk.com/our-green-pledge

# CONTENTS

| | |
|---|---|
| **INTRODUCTION** | 4 |
| **HOW TO DETECT A PREDATOR** | 6 |

### CLEVER CAMOUFLAGE — 8

| | |
|---|---|
| **THE DEAD LEAF DISGUISE**<br>Oak leaf butterfly | 10 |
| **CHAMPIONS OF CAMOUFLAGE**<br>Cuttlefish, algae octopus, bobtail squid | 12 |
| **HIDING IN PLAIN SIGHT... AND SMELL**<br>Harlequin filefish | 14 |

### SAFER TOGETHER — 16

| | |
|---|---|
| **THE LANGUAGE OF DANGER**<br>Meerkats, crested pigeon | 18 |
| **THE DREAM TEAM**<br>Pistol shrimp, goby | 20 |
| **DEFENSIVE DANCING**<br>Starlings | 22 |

### NATURAL ARMOUR — 24

| | |
|---|---|
| **BECOMING A BALL**<br>Pangolin, armadillo lizard, trilobite | 26 |
| **ARMOUR ARCHITECTS**<br>Palmetto tortoise beetle, caddisfly | 28 |

### WARNING! — 30

| | |
|---|---|
| **SENDING OUT THE BAT SIGNAL**<br>Garden tiger moth, firefly | 32 |
| **BEAUTIFULLY DEADLY**<br>Poison frogs | 34 |

| | |
|---|---|
| INDEX | 78 |
| ACKNOWLEDGEMENTS | 80 |

## SNEAKY TRICKS — 36

**HOVER-LIES** — 38
Hoverfly

**MAKE LIKE A SNAKE** — 40
Hawk moth caterpillar, burrowing owl

**DEAD CLEVER** — 42
Hognose snake, possum

## FIGHT! — 44

**FROM THE JAWS OF DEATH** — 46
Forktail blenny

**BEWARE OF THE BOTTOM** — 48
Striped & spotted skunk, pinacate beetle

## THE GREAT ESCAPE — 50

**RUNNING ON WATER** — 52
Basilisk lizard

**ROLLING OUT OF DANGER** — 54
Golden wheel spider, pebble toad

**FLYING WITHOUT WINGS** — 56
Flyingfish, neon flying squid

**LEAVING BITS BEHIND** — 58
Five-lined skink, fish-scale gecko

## PROTECTIVE PARENTS — 60

**SAFE SHELTERS** — 62
Green lacewing, cape penduline tit

**ATTENTION-GRABBING PARENTS** — 64
Ringed plover

## PLANT POWER — 66

**PLANT OR PEBBLE?** — 68
Lithops

**PLANTS AND ANTS FOREVER** — 70
Whistling thorn acacia, bittersweet nightshade

**CHEMICAL WEAPONS** — 72
Conifers, stinging nettles

## SURVIVAL — 74

**TRAVELLING SEEDS** — 76
Chilli plants, fruit bat

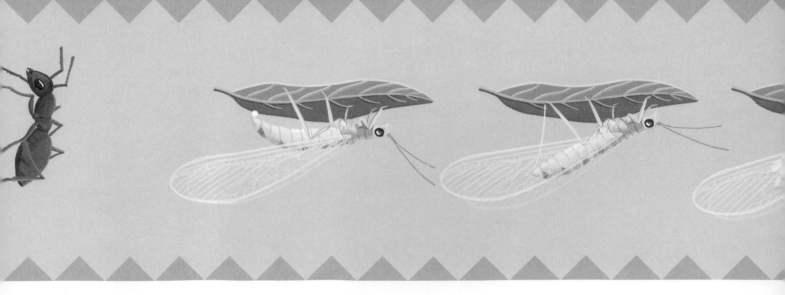

# INTRODUCTION

Life can be a dangerous business for many animals. Unless they want to end up on a predator's menu, they must develop some survival tactics. And there are ingenious tactics galore in the animal kingdom! While some animals scare their attackers into backing down, others confuse them with a fancy dance routine. Many go it alone, others team up to defeat a common foe. Some fight, some take flight – or even do a bit of both. There's no single way to stay alive, and animals cleverly play to their strengths.

And what about plants? Unable to run away or kick their enemies in the face, they're surely helpless against herbivores! Actually, plants aren't so different from animals in the way they defend themselves. From growing armour to playing mind games, they have more moves than you might think – including some outright violent ones.

Do these defences always work? Well, no. Animals and plants are guzzled every day, despite their best efforts, but that's not such a bad thing. Everyone has to eat after all. And predators can help to maintain the right balance in an ecosystem, ensuring that no individual species gets too numerous and takes over.

But predators *are* often thwarted by their intended food, and sometimes in very surprising ways...

# HOW TO DETECT A PREDATOR

If they want to remain uneaten, animals need to keep an eye out for trouble. Or a nose, ear, or indeed any other body part...

## HUMBUG DAMSELFISH

Many fish (including this stripy, coral reef dweller) make use of the nostrils on their heads to sniff out danger before it swims right up to them.

## HARBOUR SEALS

Some harbour seals not only listen out for orcas, but can distinguish between the calls made by familiar, fish-eating whales and those made by seal-eating ones!

## REINDEER

Unlike humans, reindeer (also known as caribou) can see ultraviolet light. Wolf fur absorbs this light and so will appear dark and very detectable against a snowy background.

# WOODCOCK

A woodcock's big eyes are located far back and high up on its head. Even when busy feeding, this bird can spot a predator (like an owl or weasel) coming from any direction.

# LADYBIRDS

Sometimes, plant-eating goats accidentally hoover up insects while feeding. But ladybirds can sense the heat and humidity of mammal breath, giving them a chance to escape!

# CRICKETS

A cricket has two cerci sticking out the end of its abdomen. Each of these antennae-like structures is covered in hundreds of tiny hairs, which can sense air movements produced by any predators trying to sneak up on the cricket!

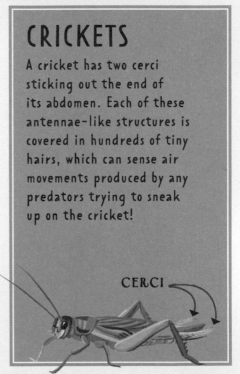

CERCI

ADULT TAPIR

BABY TAPIR

## ANTI-CAT CAMOUFLAGE

Stripy and spotty tapir babies look quite different to their mums and dads. Young tapirs are more vulnerable to wild cats, and these markings help them blend in with their sun-dappled forest home.

BITTERN

## BECOME THE REEDS

Camouflage is not just about looks – sometimes you have to act the part, too. With its streaky body, a bittern effortlessly matches its reedbed habitat. But if it spots a predator, this crafty bird can make itself look even more plant-like by pointing its beak skyward. And on breezy days it sways from side to side, just like the reeds!

# CLEVER CAMOUFLAGE

A predator can't eat something it doesn't know is there, right? By using clever camouflage, animals can get on with their business – whether that's eating, finding a mate, or snoozing – without worrying about being detected or recognised.

PARDALOTE

Fossils prove that camouflaged animals have existed for over a hundred million years. Even some dinosaurs used this anti-predator strategy!

BIRD-DROPPING SPIDER

## LIFE-SAVING FUR

Evolution has given rock pocket mice the best chance of avoiding the beady gaze of hunting owls. Most of these North American rodents have light-coloured fur to match the pale rocks they live among. But some of the mice live on black volcanic rock, and have evolved darker, better-camouflaged fur.

ROCK POCKET MOUSE

## THE GREAT POOTENDER

*Celaenia excavata* is known as the bird-dropping spider because, with its legs tucked up tight, it looks just like a splodge of bird poo. Predators (including birds themselves) are not likely to be tempted by this! The spider must stay very still for the camouflage to work – a walking poo would only raise suspicions – so it rests during the day and hunts its own prey under the cover of darkness.

# THE DEAD LEAF DISGUISE

If a predator is on the hunt for a meaty meal, a leaf is not going to make its mouth water, and a dead leaf is even less appealing! No wonder some animals have gone full leaf to fool their enemies.

## NOW YOU SEE ME

Oak leaf butterflies, found in eastern and southern Asia, are beautifully vibrant insects... some of the time. With their wings folded up they definitely do not look like delicious snacks. Unsurprisingly, they're also known as dead leaf butterflies!

Masquerade is a form of camouflage where an animal appears to be an object like a twig or leaf. It doesn't matter if the predator sees the animal, as long as it doesn't recognise it as something it can eat.

OAK LEAF BUTTERFLY (WINGS OPEN)

## THE PERFECT OUTFIT

The British naturalist Alfred Russel Wallace observed these butterflies in the 19th century and thought their camouflage was 'absolutely perfect'. Their appearance supported a theory developed by both Wallace and fellow naturalist Charles Darwin – evolution by natural selection. Better camouflaged butterflies are more likely to survive and pass on their genes to their offspring. Over many generations, their leafy disguise has become more and more convincing.

## SPOT THE DIFFERENCE

Not only do the wings appear leaf-like in colour and shape, they have convincing markings too. A leaf's midrib (the line running down the middle) and its veins (the smaller lines across its surface) are faithfully copied, while dark splotches on the wing surface mimic the fungus often found on decaying leaves. Some butterflies even have markings that look like tiny holes!

Location is everything. The butterflies usually rest amongst dead leaves where their camouflage will be most effective.

OAK LEAF BUTTERFLY (WINGS CLOSED)

## TRIPLETAIL FISH

Young tripletails live in coastal areas close to mangrove trees, which regularly drop their dead, yellowing leaves into the water. Seizing the opportunity for disguise, the fish swims to the surface and lies on its side next to the fallen leaf. Nothing to see here... just two floating leaves! Tripletails use this strategy both to avoid the attention of predators, and to ambush their own prey.

# CHAMPIONS OF CAMOUFLAGE

Move over insects, step aside spiders... there's one group of marine molluscs who have turned camouflage into an art form!

Cuttlefish and octopuses can change their texture by pulling in or pushing out little bumps on their skin called papillae, becoming smooth or lumpy as necessary!

## QUICK CHANGE

Cuttlefish, squids, and octopuses are members of the cephalopod family, and are famous for being able to change their body colour and pattern within milliseconds. They have thousands (sometimes millions!) of organs called chromatophores in their skin, which are basically little bags full of colour. A cephalopod expands or contracts the chromatophores to release this colour or make it disappear.

COMMON CUTTLEFISH

## ELECTRICAL CAMOUFLAGE

While a shark may not be able to see a camouflaged cephalopod, this predator's head is packed full of receptors to detect the electrical signals given off by prey. If a common cuttlefish sees a shark approaching, the crafty creature reduces its breathing, covers up its bodily openings, and remains still, masking the signals drifting out of its body!

## COOL YOUR JETS

It's always good to have a plan B, and many cephalopods use jet propulsion to dramatically escape from predators. But the tiny algae octopus has a more subtle tactic. To escape without abandoning its impressive camouflage, this species can walk away from danger!

Walking backwards along the seabed on two of its arms, the octopus looks like nothing more than drifting algae.

ALGAE OCTOPUS

## BACTERIAL BUDDIES

The thumb-sized Hawaiian bobtail squid spends its nights swimming around shallow waters looking for food. To remain invisible to predators, it gets some help... from bacteria! These bacteria live within a special organ inside the squid and are bioluminescent – they have the amazing ability to give off their own light.

## GO WITH THE GLOW

This light streams out of their host's underside, allowing the squid to blend in with the glow from the moon and stars. The squid can control these light levels, so on brighter nights it glows brighter too! In return for their important service, the squid produces nutrients for the bacteria to eat.

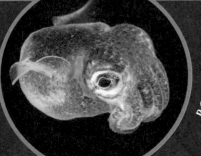

BOBTAIL SQUID

# HIDING IN PLAIN SIGHT... AND SMELL

Many animals look like something their predators find uninteresting, but surely the predators will still be able to smell them? Sometimes... not always.

An animal that eats coral, like the harlequin filefish, is called a corallivore.

## CRUCIAL CORAL

In the Indian and Pacific Oceans, dazzling harlequin filefish spend much of their time eating polyps – tiny, tentacled creatures which can gather in their thousands to form coral reefs. Coral provides the key to the harlequins' incredible anti-predator defence.

## SLEEPING SAFELY

When the day is done, the harlequin adopts a special sleeping position to prevent being munched in the night. Fixing itself to the coral, it smooths back its fins to look less fishy. With its pale tail pointing upwards and those polka dots on display, the harlequin now appears more coral than fish.

## ONE MORE TRICK

It's not just the harlequin's appearance that helps keep it hidden from predators. Lots of predators hunt by sniffing out their prey, but thanks to its coral-rich diet, this fish actually smells like coral too! When harlequins hide in the coral they have been feeding on, predatory cod can't detect their scent. Using smell to hide like this is called chemical camouflage.

SOCKEYE SALMON SMOLTS

BULL TROUT

JAPANESE HONEYBEES

## TRAVEL BUDDIES

Millions of young sockeye salmon (known as smolts) migrate from Chilko Lake in Canada to the Pacific Ocean every spring, meeting many hungry mouths along the way. But scientists tracking these youngsters found they are much more likely to survive if they travel together. Faced with a huge group of prey there's only so many the local predators can eat, and some smolts make it through.

# SAFER TOGETHER

While some animals can take care of themselves, living with others has many benefits when it comes to remaining uneaten. Not only do groups often spot predators sooner, they can even threaten, evade, or attack them together!

## OVEN-BAKED HORNET

Japanese honeybees will ruthlessly defend themselves and their hive from an invading giant hornet. Hundreds of them surround the predator, trapping it inside a bee ball before turning up the heat. By vibrating their flight muscles the bees can raise the temperature inside the ball to a scorching 46°C (115°F), killing the hornet!

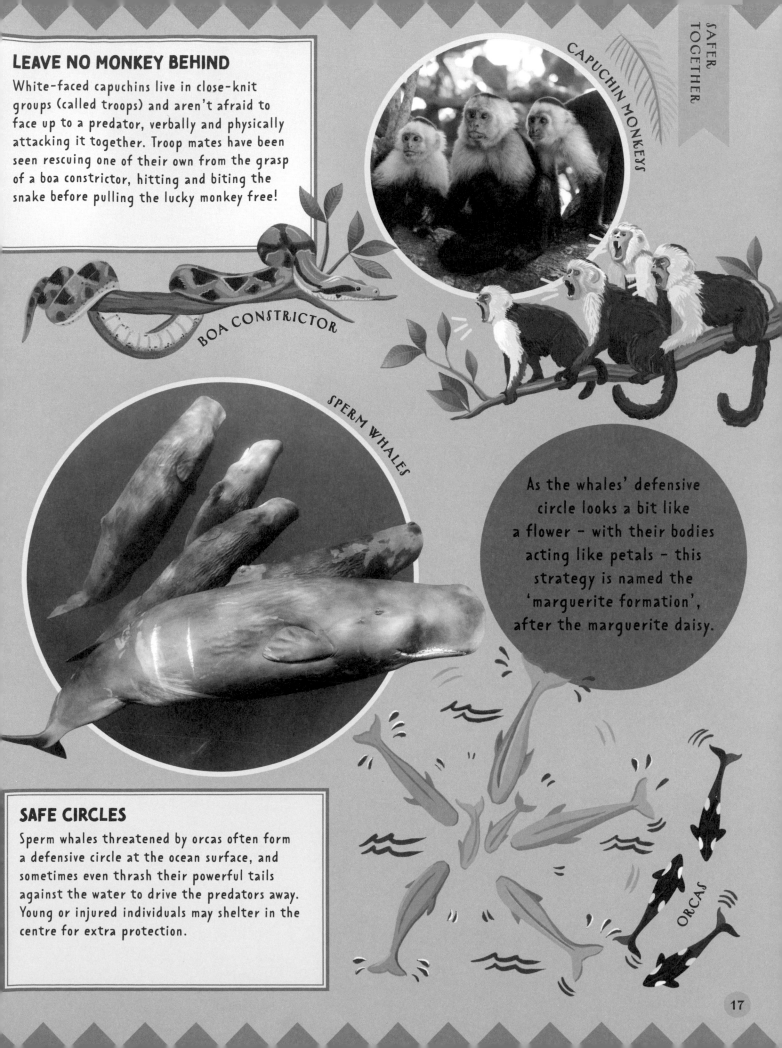

## LEAVE NO MONKEY BEHIND

White-faced capuchins live in close-knit groups (called troops) and aren't afraid to face up to a predator, verbally and physically attacking it together. Troop mates have been seen rescuing one of their own from the grasp of a boa constrictor, hitting and biting the snake before pulling the lucky monkey free!

CAPUCHIN MONKEYS

BOA CONSTRICTOR

SPERM WHALES

As the whales' defensive circle looks a bit like a flower – with their bodies acting like petals – this strategy is named the 'marguerite formation', after the marguerite daisy.

## SAFE CIRCLES

Sperm whales threatened by orcas often form a defensive circle at the ocean surface, and sometimes even thrash their powerful tails against the water to drive the predators away. Young or injured individuals may shelter in the centre for extra protection.

ORCAS

# THE LANGUAGE OF DANGER

For animals who hang out with others, it's only polite to share the news that a predator is nearby.

## HEADS IN THE SAND

Meerkats spend up to eight hours every day digging for insects and scorpions in the southern African sand. With their heads down it's not easy to detect predators, and there are plenty of those about – from jackals and wild cats on the ground to eagles up above. Luckily, meerkats are social creatures and can rely on each other to stay safe.

## GUARD KAT

Meerkats take turns to stop foraging and go on guard (or sentinel) duty, typically watching for danger for a few minutes at a time before swapping over. The sentinel climbs up to a raised position to get a better view and, if it spies trouble, calls out to warn the rest of the group. Meerkat alarm calls are incredibly varied and complex, often containing information on the type of predator and even how far away it is!

## TIME TO BOLT

The group responds to different alarms in different ways. On hearing an urgent call they race for shelter – meerkats have over a thousand boltholes scattered throughout their territory that they can dive down when necessary.

## STAND AND STARE

In less dangerous situations (like a predator walking in the distance) they may just stand on their hind legs and remain alert.

## THE SONG OF SAFETY

Sentinels even let the others know when predators aren't around. They make soft, regular calls, which is meerkat for 'Everything's fine, everyone can carry on eating!' This is known as the watchman's song.

MEERKAT SENTINEL

## CRESTED PIGEON

The Australian crested pigeon warns others by whistling, though not with its beak. Two of its flight are very narrow and produce a high-pitched whistling sound as the bird takes to the air. The faster the wings flap, the faster and louder the sound is. So as one pigeon hastily flees from a predator, its fellow pigeons are alerted to the danger and can escape too!

A meerkat group is also known as a mob, and may contain as many as 50 individuals.

# THE DREAM TEAM

Animals don't even have to be the same species to benefit from having each other around! Very different creatures, each with their own abilities, can team up to achieve a common goal... survival.

## KEEPING IN TOUCH

While the shrimp is feeding or doing important burrow repairs above ground, the goby positions itself at the entrance to keep watch. The shrimp keeps an antenna on its partner at all times, and if the goby spots a predator nearby, it flicks its tail to let the shrimp know.

## SHARING THE LOAD

Several species of pistol shrimp have developed some fishy friendships. The shrimp spends much of its time tending to its seabed burrow, which it usually shares with a goby. Although the goby doesn't help with the digging duties at all, it more than makes up for it in other ways. While the shrimp is practically blind, the goby has excellent vision and effectively acts as the shrimp's eyes.

## SCUTTLING TO SAFETY

The shrimp feels the warning flick and scuttles inside! The goby may follow its burrow-mate or continue to keep its beady eyes on the predator.

## GOING UNDERGROUND

It's far too dangerous to go wandering around in the dark, so as the sun fades, the shrimp and goby hunker down underground. The shrimp even seals the entrance so they're safely tucked in. In the morning, the goby sticks its head through the sand to open up the burrow once more.

GOBY

SHRIMP

Each burrow may house one, two or even three shrimps, along with one or two gobies.

21

# DEFENSIVE DANCING

Some birds roost together at night, to keep warm, stay safe, and even share information. But one species has a particularly dazzling pre-roost routine.

## BEDTIME BOOGIE

Before bedtime on autumn and winter evenings, European starlings start to swoop and whirl through the sky in a breathtaking group dance only they know the moves to. Sometimes, more than a million birds take part! These flocks have inspired both awe and puzzlement amongst humans watching down below. How do the starlings do this, and why?

## ALL IN THE MIND?

Watching starlings twist and twirl together so effortlessly, you'd be forgiven for thinking they were communicating with each other mentally... in fact, one bird expert in the early 20th century suggested they might be doing exactly that! It's now thought that each bird is just matching the movement of its closest six or seven neighbours, and because they react to each other in split-second time, they appear to move as one.

Because of the sound made by all those flapping wings, starling flocks are known as 'murmurations'.

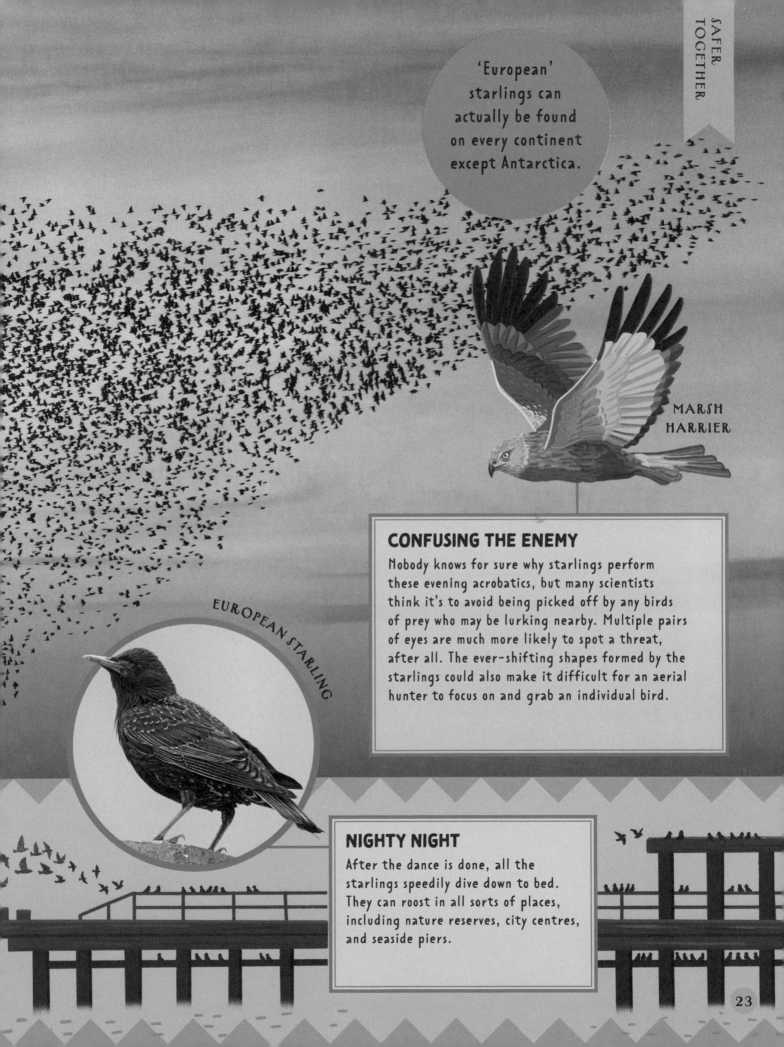

'European' starlings can actually be found on every continent except Antarctica.

MARSH HARRIER

EUROPEAN STARLING

## CONFUSING THE ENEMY

Nobody knows for sure why starlings perform these evening acrobatics, but many scientists think it's to avoid being picked off by any birds of prey who may be lurking nearby. Multiple pairs of eyes are much more likely to spot a threat, after all. The ever-shifting shapes formed by the starlings could also make it difficult for an aerial hunter to focus on and grab an individual bird.

## NIGHTY NIGHT

After the dance is done, all the starlings speedily dive down to bed. They can roost in all sorts of places, including nature reserves, city centres, and seaside piers.

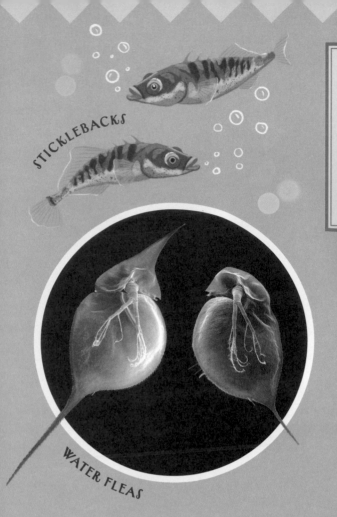

STICKLEBACKS

WATER FLEAS

## ARMOUR TO ORDER

Some water fleas use armour only when they need it most. After catching a whiff of their enemies in the water, they develop spines or helmet-like headgear! One species can grow such impressive tail and head spines that they become far too pointy for their dreaded predators, the three-spined stickleback, to handle.

# NATURAL ARMOUR

Anything that makes an animal harder to grab and swallow can only be a good thing. Sporting some natural armour – like a shell, shield, scales, or spines – could mean the difference between life and becoming lunch.

## KEEP OUT

The burrow-plug gecko puts its strange, bony tail to good use. This Australian reptile spends its days sheltering in old spider burrows with its head facing downwards and its tail sticking up like a protective shield – or plug! – to keep its enemies out.

BURROW-PLUG GECKO

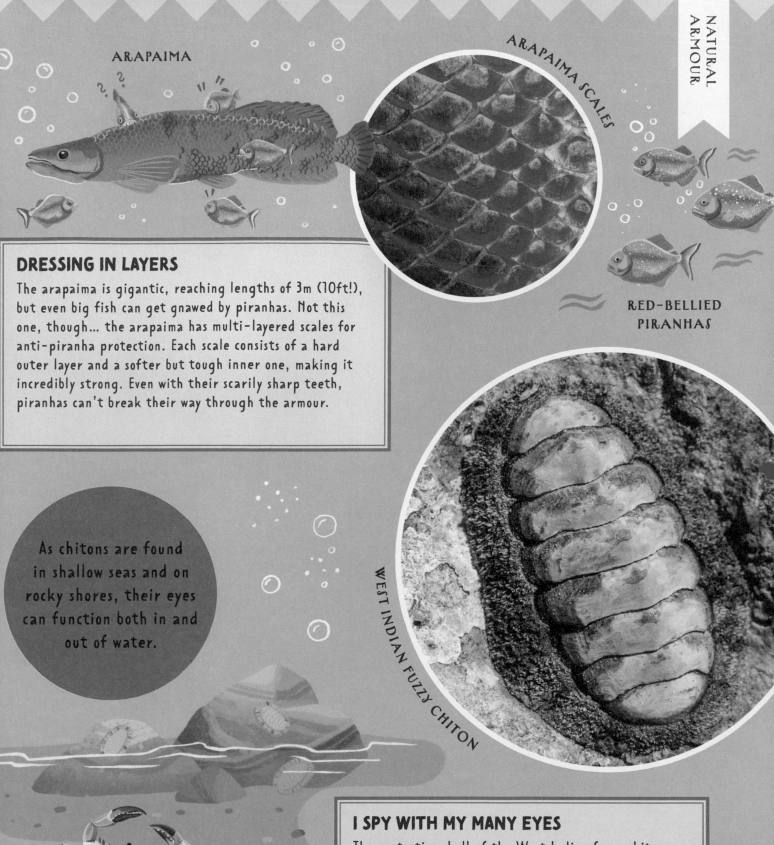

ARAPAIMA

ARAPAIMA SCALES

RED-BELLIED PIRANHAS

## DRESSING IN LAYERS

The arapaima is gigantic, reaching lengths of 3m (10ft!), but even big fish can get gnawed by piranhas. Not this one, though... the arapaima has multi-layered scales for anti-piranha protection. Each scale consists of a hard outer layer and a softer but tough inner one, making it incredibly strong. Even with their scarily sharp teeth, piranhas can't break their way through the armour.

As chitons are found in shallow seas and on rocky shores, their eyes can function both in and out of water.

WEST INDIAN FUZZY CHITON

CRAB

## I SPY WITH MY MANY EYES

The protective shell of the West Indian fuzzy chiton is studded with hundreds of miniature eyes made from the same mineral as the rest of its shell! This mollusc's vision isn't super sharp, but it can spot a predator coming from about 2m (6½ ft) away. With time to prepare, it firmly fixes itself to a rock to prevent being pulled off.

# BECOMING A BALL

By rolling up into a ball, an animal can protect its soft bits and present only its armour to a predator. This is such a successful strategy that it has evolved in lots of different species over millions of years.

PANGOLIN

## SAFE SCALES

Of all the mammals in the world, only the eight species of pangolin are truly scaly. They are almost completely covered in these sharp, overlapping scales, though a few parts – including their throats and bellies – are softer and more vulnerable. Any pangolin that senses danger will quickly hunker down into an armoured ball, forcing predators to try to unroll it... an almost impossible task.

## ARMADILLO LIZARD

The South African armadillo lizard forms a ball by biting its own tail, trusting those spiny scales to protect it from hungry mongooses. These predators find it very difficult to swallow the lizard whole when it's in this position.

## TRILOBITE

Trilobites may have been the first animals to roll into balls to avoid being eaten. They first developed over 500 million years ago, and are now extinct. But many fossils show the creatures curled up, attempting to protect their vulnerable bits with their tough exoskeletons.

## BEWARE OF THE TAIL

Any predator who does try to prise open a pangolin ball could be on the receiving end of a painful smack from the animal's scaly tail!

## WHEN IT ISN'T ENOUGH

Sadly, rolling into a ball does not protect pangolins from humans. In Asia and Africa, pangolins are hunted for their meat and their scales (which are used in traditional medicine despite having no medical value). If this doesn't stop soon, the world is in real danger of losing these unique creatures.

The word 'pangolin' comes from 'penggulung', the Malay word for 'one who rolls up'.

# ARMOUR ARCHITECTS

What if an animal isn't naturally protected with a shell or something spiky? Some ingenious species construct their own armour with whatever material they can get their hands (or bums) on.

PALMETTO TORTOISE BEETLE (ADULT)

EGG

LARVA

## NOT SOFT FOR LONG

The palmetto tortoise beetle of the southern USA lays a single egg on the frond of a palmetto plant. While she has hard wing cases, the body of her larva is soft. But soon after hatching, the larva starts to do something extraordinary... push poo out in long strands to create a protective shield!

## BABY BUILDER

Depending on which way it twists its rear, the new-born larva can bend the strands either to the left or the right as they emerge. It then attaches these strands to the spines sticking out of the end of its body using a glue-like substance released from its bum.

STINK BUG

Most insect predators don't even bother fighting their way through this impressive shield.

# CADDISFLY

For the first few months or even years of their lives, before transforming into flying adults, caddisfly larvae live underwater in ponds and streams. These can be dangerous places, so many caddisfly larvae construct protective cases around their bodies using pebbles, twigs, sand grains, or even snail shells, all glued together with silk!

ADULT CADDISFLY

The larvae grow under their shields, emerging as fully-formed adults with no more need for their inventive armour.

PALMETTO TORTOISE BEETLE (LARVA)

29

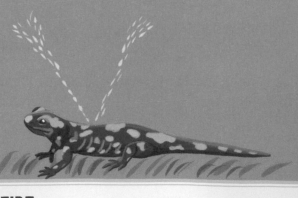

FIRE SALAMANDER

## FOREST FIRE

Fire salamanders can defend themselves by squirting toxins from their skin, a fact they advertise with their brightly patterned bodies. While it was once believed they could live in fire (hence their name) these amphibians actually shelter under logs and in other shady woodland spots, popping out only at night and on rainy days. Even in gloomy light, their cautionary colours likely grab the attention of potential predators.

MONARCH BUTTERFLY

# WARNING!

To prevent an attack, many animals warn their enemies that they're nasty-tasting or just plain dangerous. Predators learn to associate unpleasant prey with bold, contrasting colours – or even distinctive smells and sounds – and avoid them.

MONARCH CATERPILLARS ON MILKWEED

## TOXIC WINGS

Monarch butterfly caterpillars eat only milkweed, a highly poisonous plant most other animals can't tolerate. The toxins are stored in the monarchs' bodies and stay there even after their transformation into adult butterflies. The dazzling appearance of these insects hint at their dark side... birds which eat them may throw up!

BROWN TREE SNAKE

HOODED PITOHUI

## A WHIFF OF DANGER

The hooded pitohui is one of the world's few poisonous birds. As well as sporting that striking look, it gives off an icky stink which may serve as a warning to predators that its skin and feathers are packed with toxins. People who share the island of New Guinea with the pitohui call it the rubbish bird!

The strategy of sending out an honest warning to predators to stay away is called aposematism, which comes from the Greek words for 'away' and 'sign'.

LEOPARD

## PRICKLY PREY

A black and white outfit can indicate a tricky meal, and you don't get much trickier than a porcupine. This colour scheme only draws more attention to those fearsome quills. If the sight weren't alarming enough, these feisty rodents may also rattle their tail quills menacingly to hammer the message home.

PORCUPINE

The night-flying garden tiger moth is just one of about 11,000 species of tiger moth!

# FIREFLY

Many fireflies are capable of producing light from their abdomens, but why? It's long been known that these insects use their beautiful bioluminescence to attract mates, but shining bright may also serve to warn bats of their toxic bodies! While bats are experts at hunting with sound, they're certainly not blind – they can spot those lit-up rears, recognise them as danger signs, and steer clear.

# SENDING OUT
# THE BAT SIGNAL

Many bats are voracious hunters of insects, but they
really don't want to be chomping down on
unpleasant-tasting, or even harmful, ones.
If only there were some way of knowing
which insects to avoid...

PIPISTRELLE

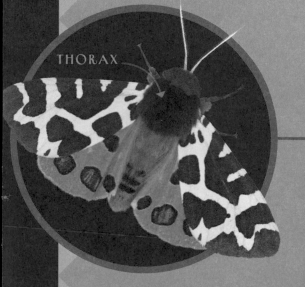

THORAX

## EAVESDROPPING INSECTS

Many bats hunt using echolocation. By sending out bursts
of high-frequency clicks and listening to the echoes that
bounce back (a technique called echolocation), bats can
detect food in the darkness. And bats need lots of food – a
single pipistrelle can hoover up 3,000 insects in one night!
But as the bats click away, some of these insects are listening
in. Garden tiger moths have ears on their thorax, and can
hear the bats heading their way.

## A MOTH'S MESSAGE

These moths not only hear their
enemies but can reply to them too.
By contracting and relaxing muscles
connected to their tymbals (sound-
producing organs on the thorax) they
blast out their own high-frequency
clicks. Garden tigers are full of toxins,
and these clicks could be their way of
warning bats, 'Don't eat me, I'm not
a delicious snack!' Bats seem to get
the message loud and clear, linking
the revolting taste of toxic moths
with those warning sounds and avoiding
them. Everybody wins!

# BEAUTIFULLY DEADLY

Why blend in when you can stand out? Some animals take this motto to extremes, trusting in their snazzy appearance to ward off danger.

GOLDEN POISON FROG

## SMALL BUT MIGHTY

The poison frogs of Central and South America may be tiny but they're far from defenceless. Many species have toxic chemicals in their skin that make them taste foul and may even be lethal to predators. These frogs' bright bodies act like warning beacons to those who hunt by sight, like birds, which is useful for all concerned – birds avoid nibbling something nasty, while the frogs remain unnibbled.

## STEP AWAY FROM THE FROG

At just 5cm (2in) long, the golden poison frog is actually one of the larger species. It also ranks among the most poisonous animals in the world, with enough toxins in just one frog to kill ten humans!

## POISON PINCHERS

Poison frogs snack on toxic minibeasts like ants and mites, but seem to suffer no ill effects. Instead, they take the poisons and store them in their skin glands, ready for use against their own predators! Frogs kept in zoos are not poisonous because they don't have the same toxic diet.

STRAWBERRY POISON FROG

## LISTEN UP, LADIES

Poison frogs' bold bodies allow them to act boldly too. They're not afraid to go out in the forest during the day, or to make plenty of noise. No cowering in the leaf litter trying not to rustle for this strawberry poison frog – he needs to call for a mate. Perched high on a log or leaf he belts out his song, hopefully attracting the attention of a female frog looking (and listening) for love. Being able to sing out in the open like this without worrying about being eaten is a major benefit of that flashy outfit.

Strawberry poison frogs are also known as blue jeans frogs!

## WALK THE WALK

Ants can be hard work to hunt, often stinging, biting or spraying acid at attackers. But this is no ant... it's a spider! The cunning arachnid takes advantage of many predators' wariness towards ants by looking like one. It even copies the way they move – ants walk in zigzags as they follow trails of chemicals left by others, so this spider walks the same way.

ANTS

Hundreds of spider species have evolved to be ant imposters.

# SNEAKY TRICKS

While honesty may be the best policy for some animals, others seem determined to lie their way out of becoming a meal. Sneaky tricks can be deployed to repel, confuse or even scare the metaphorical pants off a predator.

## LARGE AND IN CHARGE

Convincing a predator that they're larger than they really are – and therefore too dangerous to tackle – is a classic animal trick. Many owls are masters at it, and even young owlets know how it works. They fluff up their feathers, spread their wings, and sometimes sway around and clatter their beaks for good measure.

LONG-EARED OWL

## FEARSOMELY FRILLY

Terrifying, no? Actually... no, not really. The frilled lizard of Australia and New Guinea is more of a bluffer than a fighter. When in danger, its best bet is to open its mouth, fan out its neck frill, and do a bit of angry hissing. This may persuade a predator that the lizard is too big and scary to eat – or at least make it hesitate, allowing the lizard to run away!

FRILLED LIZARD

PIED FLYCATCHER

PEACOCK BUTTERFLY

## LOOK INTO MY EYES

Peacock butterflies usually keep their wings shut when resting (giving off a dead leaf vibe) but if a predator approaches, they flick them open to reveal 'eyes'. These markings are known as eyespots and are useless for seeing with... but not for scaring with. The eyes certainly seem to put off some small, insect-eating birds, who perhaps fear they belong to their own predators – bigger birds!

# HOVER-LIES

Many bees and wasps are armed with stingers that can be wielded in self-defence, making some predators think twice before attacking. But not everything dressed like an unappealing animal is the real deal.

The strategy of copying a more dangerous or yucky animal is known as Batesian mimicry, named after the Victorian explorer Henry Bates who studied this crafty defence.

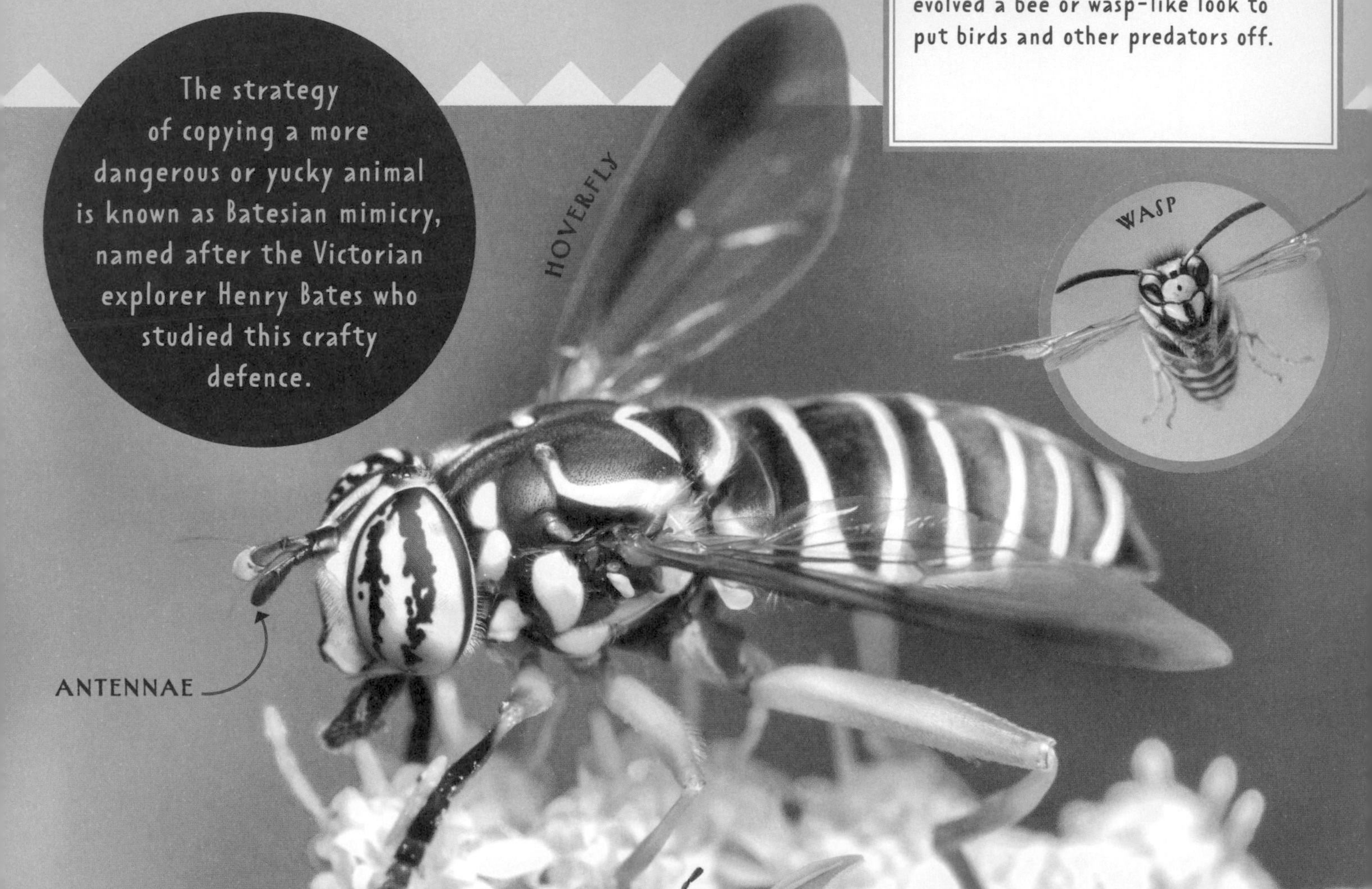

HOVERFLY

WASP

ANTENNAE

While wasps typically have long antennae, hoverflies are often a bit lacking in this area...

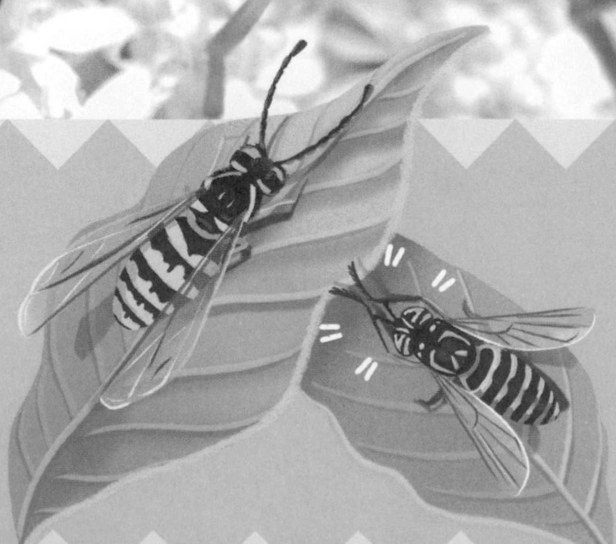

...so, to give the impression of two impressive antennae, some hoverflies waggle their dark front legs in front of their heads!

BUMBLEBEE

HOVERFLY

## FURRY FAKER

Bumblebees are covered in thick hair, giving them a furry look – just like this sneaky individual, who is nothing more than a hoverfly wearing a bee outfit! At first glance it appears very convincing. For a predator looking for a snack that won't sting them in the face, the risk of grabbing something that might turn nasty can be too high... the fly may just live to fly another day.

## HELPFUL HOVERFLIES

Hoverflies can be unpopular with people too, who fear getting stung just as much as predators do. But hoverflies, like both bees and wasps, are important plant pollinators and should be celebrated!

Like all true flies, hoverflies have two wings. Real bees and wasps have four.

39

# MAKE LIKE A SNAKE

The last thing many animals on the search for a meal want to see – or hear – is a scary snake. So a snake-like disguise can be very handy indeed...

### WHEN PLAN A FAILS

While camouflage can be useful, it's not foolproof. This hawk moth caterpillar usually blends in amongst the forest vegetation, but can raise its game if discovered by a bird or another predator.

### SHOWTIME

Keeping its bum end in place, the caterpillar tips the rest of its body backwards to really put on a show.

### WHEN DINNER TURNS DEADLY

By puffing up its front end the caterpillar reveals two striking marks on its underside which look frighteningly like a pair of eyes glinting in the sunlight. The upside down caterpillar is transformed into a dangerous snake eyeballing its dinner, hopefully making the predator flee.

The caterpillar sways around and lunges at its enemies to appear even more snake-like!

HAWK MOTH CATERPILLAR

## DARING OWL-BUTTERFLY

When it's time to turn into an adult, a daring owl-butterfly caterpillar attaches itself to a suitable plant and sheds its old skin. Here it hangs within its new, hard skin (the chrysalis) for a couple of weeks. This can be a vulnerable stage in its life - you can't escape from predators when you're busy transforming - so having a chrysalis which looks like a scary snake head is a definite plus. The chrysalis even joggles around when touched!

DARING OWL-BUTTERFLY CHRYSALIS

RATTLESNAKE

## BURROWING OWL

Burrowing owls nest underground, often in old rodent burrows. They face many enemies, including cats, weasels, and badgers. Venomous rattlesnakes are known for loudly rattling their tails to warn their own enemies to back off, and burrowing owls make a very similar sound! If a predator gets too close to a burrow but hasn't yet seen the feathery owner, the owl opens its beak and unleashes its rattle-like hiss. Fear of getting bitten may send the predator packing.

41

## POSSUM

If grabbed by a predator, a possum may topple over, drool, wee, poo, and release stinky fluid from its anal glands. Has the poor animal fainted through shock, or is it all part of a cunning plan to confuse and disgust its enemy? Nobody knows for sure! But sometimes the death act does seem to put the predator off (perhaps it's the smell). Possums are so famous for this anti-predator tactic that playing dead is often known as 'playing possum'.

# DEAD CLEVER

While it may seem risky, some animals in danger pretend to be dead! All sorts of animals have been known to do it, including frogs, stick insects, beetles, ducks, and lizards. It's often attempted when all else has failed – a final, desperate (and slightly odd) effort to stay alive.

## INFLATING SNAKE

When faced with a threat, a hognose snake may first try to make itself look much bigger and more threatening by flattening its head and neck and puffing up its body. It may also hiss and lunge at the attacker but rarely bites, preferring to save its fangs for its prey. If this doesn't work the snake throws itself into a dramatic death routine.

Scientists have observed young hognose snakes playing dead, suggesting they're born willing and able to defend themselves this way.

HOGNOSE SNAKE

## AND THE OSCAR GOES TO...

While violently wriggling around as if terribly ill, the snake may also poo and regurgitate its food. It ends up on its back with its tongue out, looking and smelling rather unappetising. Sometimes blood oozes from its mouth to add to the deathly illusion.

## BACK FROM THE DEAD?

Once the threat has passed, the snake simply rights itself and carries on with its day, seemingly resurrected from the dead. It's not surprising that hognoses have been called zombie snakes!

43

DESERT KANGAROO RAT

## GYMNASTIC ATTACK

A desert kangaroo rat may seem like an easy meal for a rattlesnake lying in wait, but this feisty rodent has a secret weapon – two, in fact. As the hunter strikes, the rat leaps and twists in the air, kicks the snake away with its huge hind legs, and bounds off. Speed, power, and agility are crucial if the rat is to avoid being pumped full of venom.

# FIGHT!

Many animals don't take being eaten lying down. They fight for their lives with whatever weapons they've got, whether that's sharp fangs, mighty limbs, or disgusting bodily fluids.

TEXAS HORNED LIZARD

BOBCAT

## BLEURGH!

A Texas horned lizard can squirt its own blood out of its eyes, right into a predator's mouth! This strategy is usually deployed against feline and canine enemies like bobcats and foxes, who seem to find the taste utterly repulsive. Once squirted, the predator usually shakes its head and sticks out its tongue to clear the blood away!

## FOUL FULMARS

Northern fulmars vomit on their enemies, shooting out stinky stomach oil for up to 3m (10ft) For birds of prey this isn't just unpleasant but potentially dangerous too – splattered all over their feathers, the oily goo can seriously hamper their ability to fly. Both chicks and adults alike practise defence by vomit.

The name 'fulmar' means 'foul gull' in the Old Norse language.

NORTHERN FULMAR

ELECTRIC EEL

## SHOCKING DEFENCE

Over three-quarters of an electric eel's body is taken up by electricity-producing organs which can generate shocks. This is handy for both stunning prey and dealing with predators. These South American fish can even leap out of the water to zap potential threats – including humans!

# FROM THE
# JAWS OF DEATH

An animal that finds itself in the mouth of another may be forgiven for giving up and accepting its inevitable doom. But life isn't over till it's over – and some animals can stage spectacular, last-minute fightbacks.

Forktail blennies are part of the poison-fang blenny family.

FORKTAIL BLENNY

## DOUBLE TROUBLE

This forktail blenny is hiding a pair of formidable weapons. Rising from its lower jaw are two long, sharp fangs, and at the base of each is a gland full of venom which flows into whatever the little fish bites. And when you share the sea with lots of creatures desperate to devour you, sometimes you do have to bite for your life.

GROUPER

If the blenny gets sucked up into a bigger fish's mouth, there's really only one thing to do...

.. chomp down on the inside of the attacker's mouth with those fearsome fangs!

## NEVER AGAIN

Blenny venom probably doesn't cause a predator pain, but it does make its blood pressure fall dramatically. The poor fish starts to tremble and its mouth dangles open, allowing the blenny to scoot out to safety! Unsurprisingly, those who experience a blenny bite learn to avoid them.

47

# BEWARE OF THE BOTTOM

Warning predators to back off is all very well, but what's an animal to do if its enemy just isn't getting the message? If needed, bottoms can become dangerous weapons.

## READY, AIM, FIRE!

A skunk can spray stinky liquid out of its bottom and into a predator's face. The noxious chemical cocktail is brewed in the two glands situated either side of the anus. When it's ready to fire, a skunk will usually point its rear at the predator, lift its tail, and twist its head round to take aim. The liquid is then discharged with great force through nozzles sticking out from the anus. The skunk can spray pretty accurately from about 3m (10ft) away!

FOX

As well as smelling awful, a dose of skunk spray can cause skin irritation, vomiting, and temporary blindness.

STRIPED SKUNK

## READ THE SIGNS

It takes days to refill the glands with liquid, so a skunk won't just spray at anyone it doesn't like the look of. It provides fair warning first in the hope it won't have to waste this precious resource. That bold black and white fur is a clear signal that this prey is not worth bothering with, and the skunk may also hiss, stomp, and growl at the predator to firmly get its point across. Only as a last resort will it spray.

SPOTTED SKUNK

## PINACATE BEETLE

Some pinacate beetles (known as desert stink bugs) also adopt the bum-in-the-air technique. As with the spotted skunks, their crobatics alone may make enemies back away. If not, the beetles shoot irritating chemicals out of their backsides. But some predators have learned to deal with this defence – a hungry grasshopper mouse will quickly shove a beetle's bum in the ground before the spray can be deployed.

## HANDSTAND AND DELIVER

Some species – the spotted skunks – have their own special warning routine... they perform a handstand! While this may not look terrifying, it clearly draws attention to that dangerous bottom and most predators take the hint. If necessary, spotted skunks can spray while in this position too, though they usually drop to all fours first.

CATERPILLAR

# THE GREAT ESCAPE

There's no shame in escaping from trouble, especially if that trouble looks hungry. From sprinting at high speed to bouncing down a mountain, there are all sorts of exit strategies in the animal kingdom.

## DIG TO SAFETY

Aardvarks spend their days in huge burrows which can reach 13m (42ft) in length. If an aardvark comes across a predator above ground it dives into a nearby burrow – or speedily digs a new one. Using its powerful claws like shovels, the aardvark can be underground within minutes.

## ABSEILING CATERPILLARS

Some caterpillars use their silk like lifelines. If one finds itself sharing a plant with something scary, it quickly drops down a silken thread spun from the spinneret near its mouth. The caterpillar dangles there until the threat is passed, before climbing back up.

AARDVARK

PRONGHORN

WOLF

## CATCH ME IF YOU CAN

The pronghorn is North America's fastest land animal. Thanks to its huge lungs and heart it can hit 95kph (60mph), easily outsprinting predators. It probably evolved this speed to escape American cheetahs – these wild cats are now extinct, but the pronghorn thrive, running rings around the much slower wolves and coyotes.

## MULTI-PURPOSE MANDIBLES

Trap-jaw ants have massive jaws (called mandibles), handy for rapidly grabbing prey. Some of these ants use them for escaping from their own fearsome predators too! Antlion larvae hunt ants by digging pits in the sand and waiting for their victims to fall in. But by smacking their mandibles hard against the ground, the ants can generate enough power to jump up and away from the pit of doom.

TRAP-JAW ANT

Some trap-jaw ants can snap their mandibles shut at an astonishing 230kph (145mph!)

ANTLION LARVA

51

# RUNNING ON WATER

Thanks to their super speed and fantastic feet, basilisk lizards have the ability to make the seemingly impossible, possible.

### DROP AND RUN

In the forests of Latin America, basilisks can often be found resting on branches above a pond or stream. They remain vigilant for snakes sneaking up the tree, and birds of prey above. If they sense danger they head right for the water, and start to run along the surface!

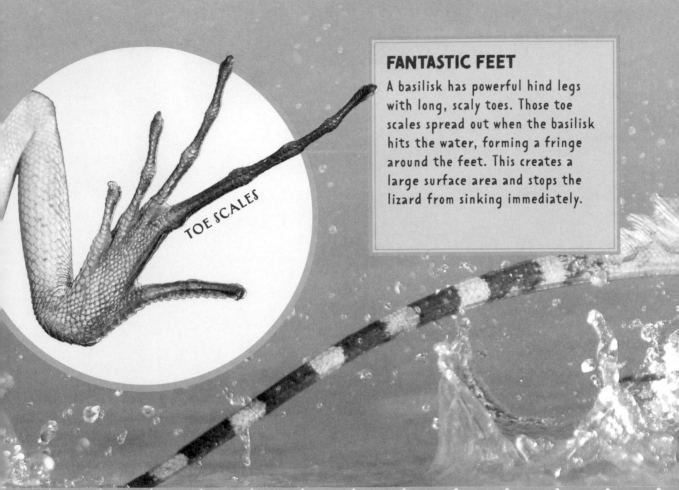

TOE SCALES

### FANTASTIC FEET

A basilisk has powerful hind legs with long, scaly toes. Those toe scales spread out when the basilisk hits the water, forming a fringe around the feet. This creates a large surface area and stops the lizard from sinking immediately.

Basilisks can bound across the water at about 2m (6½ft) a second!

SLAP

BASILISK LIZARD

All four species
of basilisk lizard
can run on water
to escape danger.

## STEADY STRIDES

As they run, basilisks slap the
water hard and stroke it down
and away, producing a bubble
of air around their feet. They
then pull their feet out of the
water before this bubble bursts,
reducing drag, and begin the
cycle again. If they do sink
before reaching land, they
may swim the rest of the
way or even hide underwater
until the threat has passed.

STROKE

RECOVER

53

# ROLLING OUT OF DANGER

You don't always need incredible running speed to be an excellent escape artist. Sometimes, letting gravity do the hard work is the safest strategy.

## DUNE DWELLERS

Within a burrow in the sloping dunes of the Namib desert in southern Africa, the golden wheel spider spends its days sheltering from the sun and staying out of trouble. But sometimes trouble breaks in...

## THE EGG OF DOOM!

A female pompilid wasp (also known as a spider wasp) is quite capable of digging a spider out of its hidey hole, and her intentions are not friendly. She's hoping to sting it and lay an egg inside its body. Her larva would then devour the spider while the poor thing is paralysed but still alive. The spider really needs to escape before this happens!

POMPILID WASP WITH SPIDER

After a bit of a run-up, the spider flips onto its side, curls up its legs...

...and simply rolls away!

# PEBBLE TOAD

Pebble toads can only be found on the summits of two flat-topped mountains in Venezuela, South America. These tiny amphibians have to get creative to escape the predatory spiders who share their mountaintop homes. When facing danger, a toad folds up its legs and rolls off the edge of the mountain like a pebble... bounce, bounce, bouncing away from the hairy grasp of its nemesis above!

Insects that lay their eggs on or inside the bodies of others are called parasitoids.

GOLDEN WHEEL SPIDER

## SPIDER SPEEDSTER

Spinning down the steep dunes is much faster and more efficient than running. The spider can reach speeds of 1.5m (5ft) per second, leaving the wasp far behind! And it's difficult for her to follow her intended victim - the spider is so light it leaves behind only very faint marks in the sand as it wheels along.

## TAXI FOR ONE

Some flyingfish can glide for around 400m (1300ft) – roughly the length of four football fields – but they need to do a bit of work to keep up the momentum. If a fish starts to descend seaward too soon, it dunks the lower fork of its tail into the water again for another quick wiggle. This is called 'taxiing' and provides enough thrust for the fish to carry on gliding.

FLYINGFISH

Scientists aren't sure how many species of flyingfish there are, but think it's probably around sixty.

## NEON FLYING SQUID

These unusual cephalopods propel themselves into the air by squirting water out of their bodies at force. Their fins and arms act like wings, allowing them to glide for over 30m (100ft) in three seconds before plopping back into the water.

# FLYING WITHOUT WINGS

The sea can be a dangerous place, so it's no surprise that some sea-dwellers are keen to leave it behind... by flying out of there! Sort of.

## TAKING OFF

If pursued by a predator, a flyingfish powers towards the surface like a fishy torpedo with its 'wings' tucked up against its side. As its body bursts free of the sea, the long, lower fork of its tail often remains underwater. The fish wiggles its tail vigorously for an extra boost, unfurls its wings, and begins to fly above the waves!

SWORDFISH

FINS

## FAST FINS

The fish's wings are, in fact, its fins. All flyingfish have huge pectoral (front) fins and many have large pelvic (rear) fins too, effectively giving them four wings. The fish can't flap them like a bird, so it doesn't so much fly as glide. But it can do so extremely quickly – up to 72kph (45mph), around twice its swimming speed.

57

# LEAVING BITS BEHIND

Before escaping, certain animals leave a part of themselves behind – an arm, leg, tail, even a patch of skin!

## MAKING A SACRIFICE

The voluntary shedding of a body bit is called autotomy and is seen in all sorts of animals, from spiders to sea stars, mice to octopuses. Lizards are particularly well-known for this strategy. The North American five-lined skink, like many of its lizard cousins, is willing and able to lose its tail to save its life.

## A CLEAN BREAK

As the predator strikes, the tail drops! It may look like the predator has torn it off, but the skink is the one running the show. Its tail contains several weak spots called 'fracture planes' – as the skink contracts the muscles around one of these spots, the tail (or part of it) snaps off. Blood vessels are sealed at the same time to prevent bleeding.

RACCOON

Five-lined skinks are born with bright blue tails, but the colour dulls with age.

FIVE-LINED SKINK

# FISH-SCALE GECKO

Off the east coast of Africa, on Madagascar and the Comoro Islands, live a group of lizards with a very special party trick. If a fish-scale gecko is grabbed, its scales and some of the skin beneath slide off in the predator's mouth! The gecko runs away and can soon regenerate its life-saving suit.

## TASTY TAIL

The detached tail can wriggle around for several minutes, distracting the predator while the skink bolts. The predator may be happy to simply guzzle the tail without bothering to give chase. But if the predator doesn't fancy the tail – or can't catch it – the skink may return later to eat it! Tails are packed full of energy so there's no point letting one go to waste.

A young five-lined skink can grow a new tail over the course of several weeks.

59

# PROTECTIVE PARENTS

Would your parents protect you if a tiger barged in looking for a snack? You can count on it! Humans are not alone in feeling an urge to protect their children. From providing the perfect shelter to chasing off predators, many animals put lots of time and effort into keeping their youngsters safe.

FIELDFARE

## MOVING HOUSE

Adult cheetahs may be top hunters, but their tiny cubs are often in danger of being eaten by bigger animals. Predators might sniff them out if they spend too long in one place, so every few days a cheetah mum grabs her cubs and carries them to a new den, one at a time.

CHEETAH

## BIRD BODYGUARDS

Fieldfares often nest close to each other and join forces to protect their young from danger. These birds have an endless supply of ammo at their disposal... they bombard predators with poo!

## POINTY PARENTS

The word 'rhinoceros' means 'horn-nosed', and rhinos have either one or two of these pointy additions to their snouts. A female rhino only has a single calf at a time and is fiercely protective of it, using her impressive weaponry to prevent predators like lions and hyenas from getting too close.

LION

Rhino horn is made from keratin, the same substance found in our hair and nails!

WASP

RHINOCEROS

THORNBUG NYMPHS

## GOOD VIBRATIONS

Young thornbugs huddle together on a plant stem for the first few weeks of their lives. If they spot a wasp these nymphs waggle their bodies to produce vibrations, which travel through the stem to their mum, on guard nearby. She senses this 'Help!' signal and goes on the attack, kicking the wasp until it retreats.

## CAPE PENDULINE TIT

The nest of southern Africa's cape penduline tit contains a very special feature – a large false entrance that leads only to a dead end, convincing any predators who barge in that there's nobody home! The real 'door' is just above the fake one. Once the parent birds have pushed it open with their feet and slipped inside, the secret entrance closes behind them.

GREEN LACEWING EGGS

# SAFE SHELTERS

A crucial part of being a good parent is providing your young with a safe place in which to start their lives, well protected from predators. This sometimes calls for a bit of creativity...

### STRONG BOND

Green lacewings have an unusual but effective egg-laying strategy. First, the adult female squeezes out a drop of liquid from her abdomen – this is her silk, which she pulls into a thin but incredibly strong thread. The thread dries in seconds and she lays an egg right at the tip of it.

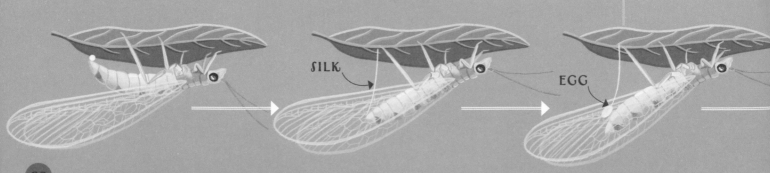

SILK

EGG

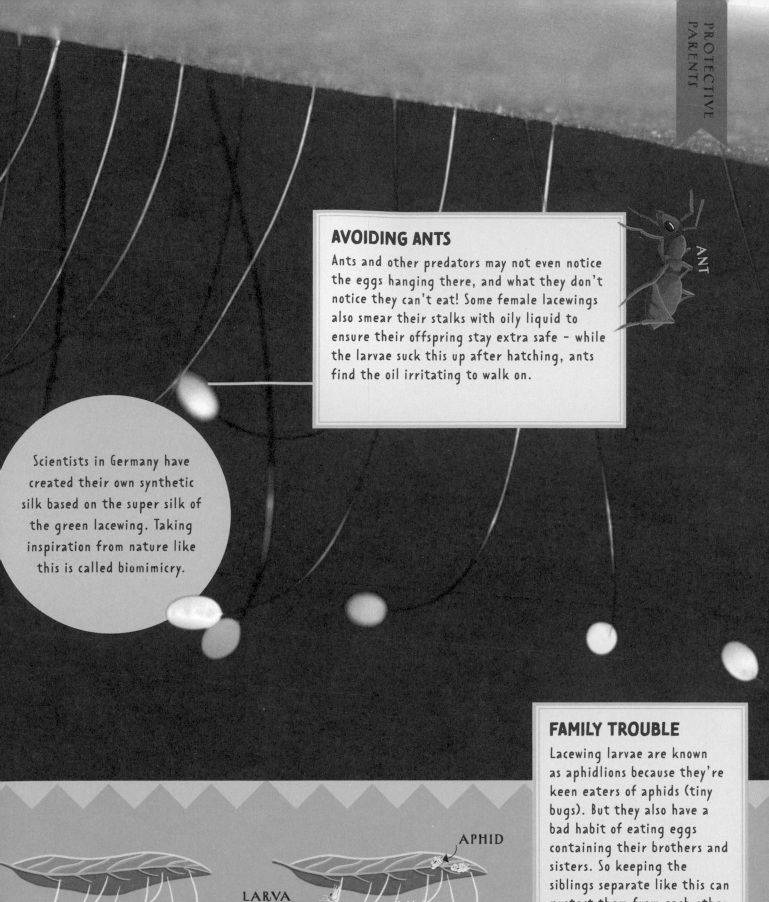

## AVOIDING ANTS

Ants and other predators may not even notice the eggs hanging there, and what they don't notice they can't eat! Some female lacewings also smear their stalks with oily liquid to ensure their offspring stay extra safe – while the larvae suck this up after hatching, ants find the oil irritating to walk on.

ANT

Scientists in Germany have created their own synthetic silk based on the super silk of the green lacewing. Taking inspiration from nature like this is called biomimicry.

## FAMILY TROUBLE

Lacewing larvae are known as aphidlions because they're keen eaters of aphids (tiny bugs). But they also have a bad habit of eating eggs containing their brothers and sisters. So keeping the siblings separate like this can protect them from each other as much as from predators.

APHID

LARVA

Lacewing eggs can often be found on leaves and twigs.

# ATTENTION-GRABBING PARENTS

Some birds are well-known for trying to drag a predator's attention away from their young ones... and on to themselves. Meet the ringed plover!

RINGED PLOVER EGGS

RINGED PLOVER

## BEACH BABIES

Nestled in a scrape on a sandy or rocky beach, the speckled eggs of the ringed plover are pretty well camouflaged. Even plover chicks blend in with the background. But a fox on the hunt is sure to discover them if it gets close enough. While it's risky nesting out in the open like this, there is one benefit – a plover parent can easily spot a predator approaching and swing into action.

RINGED PLOVER CHICK

FOX

## FOLLOW ME!

Good timing is crucial. Move too late and the fox might notice the eggs or chicks. At the right moment, the adult bobs away from the nest and begins to flutter its wings helplessly or drag one along the ground as if it were broken and useless. Injured prey makes for an easy snack, so this is bound to spark a predator's interest. Oblivious to the vulnerable nest nearby, the fox begins to follow the acting adult.

## BYE BYE BIRDIE

After leading the fox away, the plover spreads its perfectly healthy wings and simply flies back to the nest! This strategy is less likely to work with a bird of prey, who could more easily grab the adult mid-flight as it tries to escape. But there's often not much a landbound fox can do other than watch its supposedly easy snack disappear.

This strategy is known as the broken-wing display.

# PLANT POWER

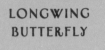

LONGWING BUTTERFLY

PASSION FLOWER

Animals aren't the only ones able to repel, trick, or attack their enemies. Plants are constantly under threat from hungry herbivores, and have developed many staying-alive strategies.

## CLOSED FOR BUSINESS

*Mimosa pudica* is sometimes called the sensitive or touch-me-not plant thanks to its ingenious defence tactic. When touched, its leaflets quickly close up! This may alarm a browsing herbivore or even send an unwanted insect tumbling off the plant.

## ANTI-EGG DEFENCE

The longwing butterfly has to lay her eggs on a passion flower, and the passion flower has to stop her if it wants to avoid being overrun by hungry caterpillars. As butterflies won't lay in a spot already covered in eggs, some passion flowers have developed little egg-like marks on their leaves! Fooled into thinking the plant is full, the butterfly flutters on.

MIMOSA PUDICA

AMAZON WATER LILY

MANATEE

## NIBBLE IF YOU DARE

At over 2m (6½ft) across, the leaves of the Amazon water lily – the largest water lily in the world – can comfortably serve as chairs for humans. But keep your bum away from the undersides of these gigantic floating pads... they're covered in pointy spines to defend against nibblers lurking beneath the water, like fish and manatees.

Over 200 species of plants trap sand, a tactic known as psammophory (Greek for 'sand-carrying').

YELLOW SAND VERBENA

## SANDY ARMOUR

Yellow sand verbenas release glue-like fluid from glands on their leaves and stems to make themselves sticky. These plants thrive in sandy habitats and as sand grains waft past on the wind they coat the verbenas, providing useful armour! A crusty plant makes for an unpleasant mouthful and can grind down a herbivore's teeth, so is best avoided.

# PLANT OR PEBBLE?

It's not just animals who can fool their enemies
with their appearance. Some plants are experts in
the art of camouflage too, masquerading as objects
the local herbivores are likely to ignore.

## JUICY TARGETS

In the rocky deserts of southern Africa, stones litter the
landscape. But some of these apparent stones are mere
pretenders... some are actually lithops. Lithops are known as
succulents (meaning 'juicy'), because their thick leaves are
perfect for storing moisture. This could make them prime
targets for herbivores craving both a snack and a drink,
so it's a good job these plants are masters of disguise.

The name 'lithops'
comes from the Greek
words, 'lithos'
('stone') and
'ops' ('face').

## BLOOMING LOVELY

The only time a lithops looks more plant-like than stone-like is when a single flower blooms from the slit between the two leaves. After the flower has faded, it's time for a change of outfit. New, stone-like leaves rise up from the slit to replace the old, shrivelled ones.

There are around 40 species of lithops and they come in various colours and patterns (just like pebbles do!)

## BURIED TREASURE

Most of a lithops is underground, with only the tips of its leaves sticking out. Translucent areas on the leaf surface act like windows, allowing sunlight to pass through to the hidden parts of the plant. Photosynthesis actually takes place beneath the surface! As well as keeping it safe from prying eyes and munching mouths, this unusual, underground way of life means the plant can conserve water and keep cool in its arid surroundings.

# PLANTS AND ANTS FOREVER

For a plant, an invasion of insects could spell trouble. But not all insects want to chew plants to death – some can even protect them from their worst enemies.

## HELPFUL HOUSEMATES

Some trees on the African savanna have a hard time against elephants. These hefty herbivores are well capable of devouring even very thorny plants, and can push whole trees over! Fortunately, the whistling thorn acacia has many live-in ant bodyguards... and they do not stand for any nonsense.

Each tree can house around 90,000 ants!

## ANTS VS ELEPHANTS

Ants patrol the tree on the alert for danger. If an elephant begins to browse, they head up the invader's trunk – a very sensitive spot – and start biting. The ants release chemicals called pheromones to signal their tree-mates to join in with the attack. By working together, these tiny insects can drive away a massive elephant!

ACACIA TREE

# BITTERSWEET NIGHTSHADE

When a bittersweet nightshade plant is nibbled, it bleeds! Rather than blood, it leaks droplets of nectar, which soon attract sugar-loving ants. The ants slurp up the nectar and, in return, act as protectors. They hunt down the flea beetle larvae trying to burrow their way into the plant, and even attack slugs to stop these nibblers in their tracks!

ANTS ON A WHISTLING THORN ACACIA

## BED AND BREAKFAST

This is a two-way relationship, and the acacia provides shelter and sustenance to its feisty defenders. At the base of some of the thorns are hollow swellings called domatia which serve as the ants' homes. The holes made by ants chewing their way into these domatia whistle as the wind blows over them, giving the whistling thorn acacia its name. The tree also oozes sugary nectar from glands on its leaves for the ants to eat.

Even just the smell of ants on a whistling thorn acacia can put an elephant off!

# CHEMICAL WEAPONS

Many plants are loaded with toxic chemicals that can put off – and sometimes even kill! – their herbivorous foes.

**BARK BEETLES**

**NORWAY SPRUCE**

## TINY THREATS

Conifer is the name given to a group of non-flowering plants, including pine and spruce trees. Many grow to huge heights and live to a ripe old age, but even mighty conifers can face danger from the tiniest of sources. Bark beetles burrow into the bark, forming tunnels in which they lay their eggs. When the larvae hatch they feast on the tree, creating their own tunnels. While most of these insects live in dead or dying trees, some can team up to destroy healthy ones.

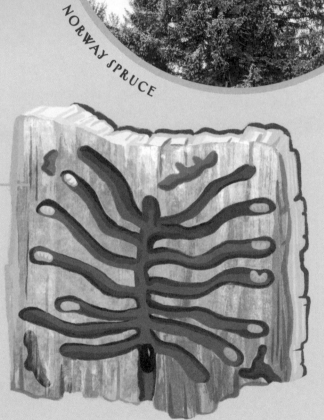

**SIKA DEER**

## STINGING NETTLES

The leaves and stems of stinging nettles are covered in tiny, sharp hairs called trichomes, which inject a cocktail of toxic, pain-inducing chemicals into anyone who brushes against them. Nara Park in Japan has been home to sika deer for over a thousand years, and while deer do eat nettles they sensibly avoid those with lots of trichomes. The park nettles are much hairier than those from nearby deer-free areas, suggesting the plants have boosted their armour to repel these troublesome munchers!

## BEWARE OF THE OOZE

Many conifers rely on resin to defend themselves from destruction. This liquid is created and stored at pressure so when a tree is wounded – by a burrowing beetle, for example – this sticky liquid oozes out. Resin is toxic to the beetles and can even drown these invaders! Once outside the tree the resin hardens, sealing the wound like a plaster.

These plants are named after their cones – 'conifer' means 'cone-bearer'.

### INSECT TRAPPED IN AMBER

Climate change is causing real problems for conifers, making some trees weaker and less able to defend themselves while allowing beetles to spread into areas once too cold for them.

## AMBER TOMBS

It's clear plants have been using the resin defence for a very long time. The oldest lump of fossilised resin (known as amber) dates from 320 million years ago! Some amber contains the preserved remains of insects and other creatures trapped forever in a tree's defensive goo, offering amazing insights into ancient life on Earth.

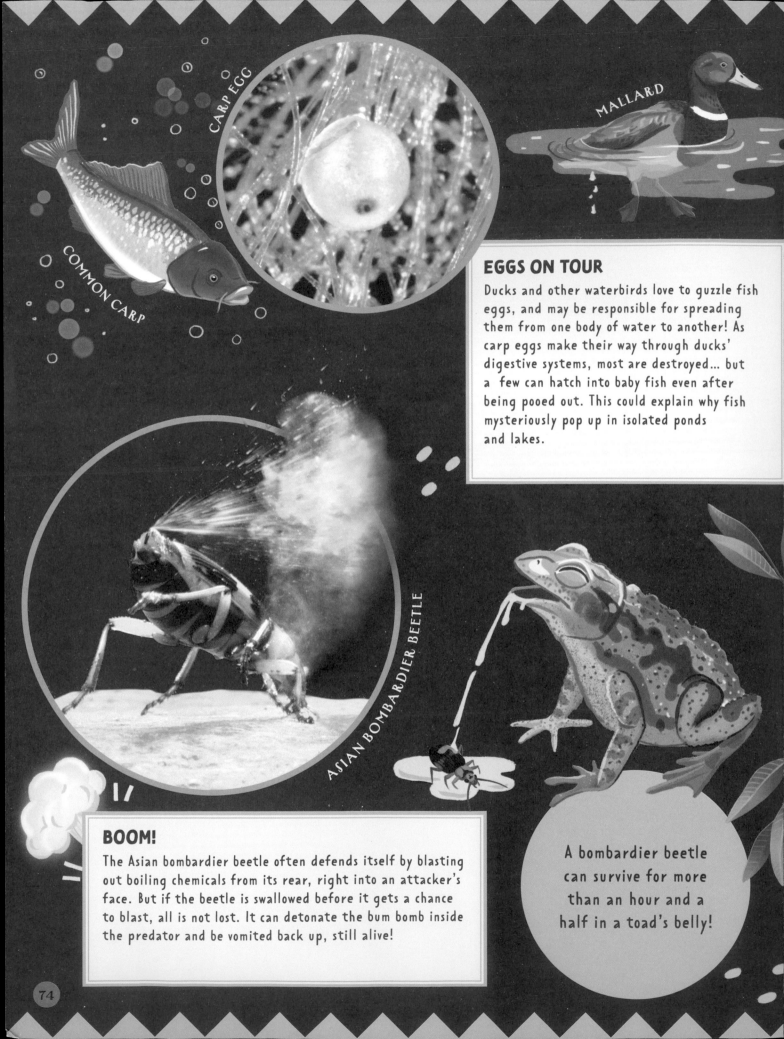

CARP EGG

MALLARD

COMMON CARP

## EGGS ON TOUR

Ducks and other waterbirds love to guzzle fish eggs, and may be responsible for spreading them from one body of water to another! As carp eggs make their way through ducks' digestive systems, most are destroyed... but a few can hatch into baby fish even after being pooed out. This could explain why fish mysteriously pop up in isolated ponds and lakes.

ASIAN BOMBARDIER BEETLE

## BOOM!

The Asian bombardier beetle often defends itself by blasting out boiling chemicals from its rear, right into an attacker's face. But if the beetle is swallowed before it gets a chance to blast, all is not lost. It can detonate the bum bomb inside the predator and be vomited back up, still alive!

A bombardier beetle can survive for more than an hour and a half in a toad's belly!

# SURVIVAL

Some animals and plants have mastered the art of surviving (and even thriving!) after being eaten, whether by returning the way they went in or enduring the rough passage from mouth to bum...

## SHUTTING THE DOOR

Some sea and freshwater snails can make it through their fishy predators in one piece. A snail simply retracts its soft bits into its shell and seals the entrance with the operculum, a handy door-like disc. All tucked up like this inside its armour, the snail is better protected from the fish's digestive juices.

ROHDE'S LEAF FROG

SEA SNAIL

WATER SNAKE

## RETURN OF THE SNACK

The one good thing about being devoured by a snake is that most of these predators swallow their food whole, sometimes when that food is still alive. If prey can survive the journey down they may just come back up intact. Like many of their amphibian cousins, Rohde's leaf frogs have unpleasant chemicals in their skin – snakes have been known to regurgitate them minutes after unwisely tucking in.

## (DON'T) FEEL THE BURN

Inside the fruits of spicy chilli plants are tiny seeds full of capsaicin, the chemical which gives the fruits their heat. Rodents can't stomach capsaicin and so keep their distance, but birds don't experience the same burning sensation that rodents (and humans!) get from eating a chilli. As the fruits ripen and turn red, birds are only too happy to get stuck in.

# TRAVELLING SEEDS

Many plants actively encourage animals to eat them, or at least part of them, in order to reproduce. While plants can't run about chucking their seeds far and wide, they can encase them inside tasty, nutritious fruit that animals will want to eat. Because what goes in must come out...

FIG

Other seed spreaders include fish, lizards, and tortoises. Seeds may actually have a better chance of growing after journeying through an animal!

# FRUIT BAT

Fruit bats guzzle various fruits, including figs and guavas, spitting out some seeds while swallowing others. By the time the swallowed seeds pop out the other end the bats are often mid-air, far away from the parent plant! Unfortunately, lots of these vital seed dispersers are threatened with extinction, and if we lose the bats we may just lose some of the plants too.

GUAVA

## GNAWERS AND GULPERS

It's no accident that chillies disgust some animals while attracting others. In a way, the plants have chosen who will eat their fruits. Rodents gnaw their food, often destroying seeds in the process, while birds, like the chilli-loving curve-billed thrasher, gulp fruits down whole. Even after being pooed out, the seeds are in great condition and able to grow.

CURVE-BILLED THRASHER

## PERCH AND POO

Birds carry seeds to new places, ensuring that seedlings won't be in competition with their parents. They also tend to go to the toilet while perched on trees or shrubs, which is ideal for chillies as they prefer growing in the shade of other plants.

# INDEX

## A

aardvarks 50
acrobatics 49
alarm calls 18
algae octopuses 13
Amazon water lilies 67
amber 73
antlions 51
ants 36, 51, 63, 70-71
aphidlions 63
aposematism 31
arapaimas 25
armadillo lizards 26
armour 24-29
autotomy 58

## B

bark beetles 72
basilisk lizards 52-53
Batesian mimicry 38
bats 32, 33, 77
bees 16, 38, 39
beetles 42, 73
  bark beetles 72
  bombardier beetles 74
  flea beetles 71
  palmetto tortoise beetles 28
  pinacate beetles 49
bioluminescence 13, 32
biomimicry 63
bird-dropping spiders 9
birds
  bitterns 8
  cape penduline tits 62
  curve-billed thrashers 77
  ducks 42, 74
  fieldfares 60
  hooded pitohuis 31
  marsh harriers 23
  northern fulmars 45
  owls 7, 36, 41
  pied flycatchers 37
  pigeons 19
  plovers 64-65
  starlings 22-23
  woodcock 7
bitterns 8
bittersweet nightshade 71
blennies 46-47
boa constrictors 17
bobcats 44
bombardier beetles 74
broken-wing display 65
bumblebees 39
burrow-plug geckos 24
burrowing owls 41
butterflies
  longwing butterflies 66
  monarch butterflies 30
  oak leaf butterflies 10-11
  owl-butterflies 41
  peacock butterflies 37

## C

caddisflies 29
camouflage 8-15, 40, 68-69
cape penduline tits 62
capsaicin 76
capuchin monkeys 17
caribou 6-7
carp 74
caterpillars 30, 40-41, 50
cephalopods 12-13, 56
cheetahs 60
chemical camouflage 14
chilli plants 76-77
chitons 25
chromatophores 12
chrysalis 41
climate change 73
conifers 72, 73
corallivores 14
crested pigeons 19
crickets 7
curve-billed thrashers 77
cuttlefish 12

## D

dance routines 22-23
Darwin, Charles 10
dead, playing 42-43
desert kangaroo rats 44
dinosaurs 9
ducks 42, 74

## E

echolocation 33
eggs 28, 54, 62-63, 64-65, 66, 72, 74
electric eels 45
elephants 70, 71
evolution 9, 10
exoskeletons 26

## F

fieldfares 60
fire salamanders 30
fireflies 32
fish
  arapaimas 25
  blennies 46-47
  carp 74
  electric eels 45
  flying fish 56-7
  gobies 20-21
  groupers 47
  harlequin filefish 14-15
  humbug damselfish 6
  piranhas 25
  salmon 16
  sharks 12
  sticklebacks 24
  tripletail fish 11
fish-scale geckos 59
five-lined skinks 58-59
flea beetles 71
flying fish 56-57

## G

geckos
  burrow-plug geckos 24
  fish-scale geckos 59
goats 7
gobies 20-21
golden poison frogs 34-35
golden wheel spiders 54-55
grasshopper mice 49
groupers 47

forktail blennies 46-47
foxes 44, 48, 65
frilled lizards 37
frogs 42
  poison frogs 34-35
  Rohde's leaf frogs 75
fruit bats 77

## H

harlequin filefish 14-15
Hawaiian bobtail squids 13
hawk moths 40
hognose snakes 42-43
honeybees 16
hooded pitohuis 31
hornets 16
hoverflies 38-39
humbug damselfish 6

## J, K

jumping spiders 36
killer whales (orcas) 6, 17

## L

lacewings 62-63
ladybirds 7
larvae 28-29, 51, 54, 63, 71, 72
lithops 68-69
lizards 42, 77

armadillo lizards 26
basilisk lizards 52-53
frilled lizards 37
geckos 24, 59
skinks 58-59
Texas horned lizards 44
ng-eared owls 36
ngwing butterflies 66

**M**

anatees 67
arsh harriers 23
asquerade 10
eerkats 18-19
ice 9, 49, 58
imosa Pudica 66
onarch butterflies 30
oths
hawk moths 40
tiger moths 32, 33
urmurations 22-23

**N, O**

on flying squid 56
rthern fulmars 45
orway spruces 72
k leaf butterflies 10-11
topuses 12, 13, 58
l-butterflies 41
ls 7, 36, 41

**P**

lmetto tortoise beetles
ngolins 26-27
pillae 12
rasitoids 55
ssion flowers 66
acock butterflies 37
bble toads 55
eromones 70
ed flycatchers 37
geons 19
nacate beetles 49
pistrelle bats 33
ranhas 25
ants 66-77

plovers 64-65
poison frogs 34-35
pompilid wasps 54
poo 9, 28, 29, 42-43, 60, 74, 77
porcupines 31
possums 42
predator detection 6-7
pronghorns 51
psammophory 67

**R**

raccoons 58
rattlesnakes 41, 44
reindeer 6-7
resin 73
rhinoceroses 61
ringed plovers 64-65
rock pocket mice 9
Rohde's leaf frogs 75

**S**

salamanders 30
salmon 16
seals 6
seeds 76-77
sharks 12
shedding body parts 58-59
shrimp 20-21
sika deer 72
skinks 58-59
skunks 48-49
smell 14-15, 31, 42, 43, 48
snails 75
snakes 31, 40, 52, 53, 75
    boa constrictors 17
    hognose snakes 42-43
    rattlesnakes 41, 44
sperm whales 17
spider wasps 54
spiders 58
    bird-dropping spiders 9
    golden wheel spiders 54-55
    jumping spiders 36
spotted skunks 49
squids 12, 13, 56
starlings 22-23
sticklebacks 24
sticky fluid 28, 63, 67, 73

stingers 38
stinging nettles 72
stink bugs 28, 49
strawberry poison frogs 35
succulents 68-69

**T**

tail, shedding 58-59
tapirs 8
Texas horned lizards 44
thornbugs 61
tiger moths 32, 33
toads 55, 74
tortoises 77
toxins and venom 30, 32, 33,
            34, 35, 46, 47, 72, 73
trap-jaw ants 51
trilobites 26
tripletail fish 11

**V, W**

verbenas 67
vomit 45, 74
Wallace, Alfred Russel 10
wasps 38, 39, 54, 61
water fleas 24
water lilies 67
weasels 7, 41
West Indian fuzzy chitons 25
whales 7, 17
whistling thorn acacias 70-71
wolves 6, 51
woodcock 7

**Y**

yellow sand verbenas 67

## ABOUT THE AUTHOR

JOSETTE REEVES is a nature-loving writer and editor from Lancashire. Her first book was *Got to Dance*, a story about a dancing monkey. This is her debut non-fiction book and is a tad more scientific. She also writes short stories and articles for children's magazines.

## ABOUT THE ILLUSTRATOR

ASIA ORLANDO is a digital artist, illustrator, and environmentalist. Asia creates artwork for books, magazines, products, and posters. Her work focuses on harmony between animals, humans, and the environment. She's also the founder of *Our Planet Week*, a social media event for illustrators aimed to address environmental issues.

# ACKNOWLEDGMENTS

The publisher would like to thank the following for their kind permission to reproduce their photographs:

(Key: a-above; b-below/bottom; c-centre; f-far; l-left; r-right; t-top)

**2 Dorling Kindersley**: Asia Orlando 2022 (bl). **3 Dorling Kindersley**: Asia Orlando 2022 (tl); Asia Orlando 2022 (br). **4-5 Dorling Kindersley:** Asia Orlando 2022 (t); Asia Orlando 2022 (b). **6-7 Dorling Kindersley:** Asia Orlando 2022 (illustrations). **6 Alamy Stock Photo:** Nature Picture Library / Alex Mustard (cl). **naturepl.com:** Alex Mustard (cr). **7 naturepl.com:** Gerrit Vyn (tr); Andy Sands (cb). **Shutterstock.com:** Mariemily Photos (bl). **8 Alamy Stock Photo:** Juniors Bildarchiv GmbH / F382 (tr). **Getty Images / iStock:** merlinpf (clb). **8-9 Dorling Kindersley:** Asia Orlando 2022. **9 Alamy Stock Photo:** Rick & Nora Bowers (br); Genevieve Vallee (cl). **10 Alamy Stock Photo:** David Carillet (c). **10-11 Dorling Kindersley:** Asia Orlando 2022. **11 Alamy Stock Photo:** Pally (bl); sablin (c). **12-13 Dorling Kindersley:** Asia Orlando 2022 (illustrations). **12 Alamy Stock Photo:** Nature Picture Library / Wild Wonders of Europe / Pitkin (b). **13 Alamy Stock Photo:** Nature Picture Library (c). **naturepl.com:** Doug Perrine (bl). **14-15 Alamy Stock Photo:** Richardom. **15 Dorling Kindersley:** Asia Orlando 2022 (r). **16-17 Dorling Kindersley:** Asia Orlando 2022. **16 © Patrick J Endres / www.AlaskaPhotoGraphics.com:** (tl). **Shutterstock. com:** feathercollector (clb). **17 Alamy Stock Photo:** Nature Picture Library / Tony Wu (cl). **Getty Images:** Moment / Kryssia Campos (tr). **18 Dorling Kindersley:** Asia Orlando 2022. **19 Alamy Stock Photo:** Minden Pictures / BIA / Greg Oakley (crb). **naturepl.com:** Klein & Hubert. **20-21 Alamy Stock Photo:** Stocktrek Images, Inc. / Bruce Shafer (b). **22-23 Alamy Stock Photo:** Arterra Picture Library / Arndt Sven-Erik (t). **Dorling Kindersley:** Asia Orlando 2022 (illustration). **23 Getty Images:** Gary Chalker (clb). **24 Dreamstime.com:** Ken Griffiths (br). **Science Photo Library:** Christian Laforsch (cla). **24-25 Dorling Kindersley:** Asia Orlando 2022. **25 Alamy Stock Photo:** Auk Archive (cr); Minden Pictures / Pete Oxford (tc). **26 Alamy Stock Photo:** Nature Picture Library / Daniel Heuclin (bc). **Dorling Kindersley:** Asia Orlando 2022. **Getty Images / iStock:** 2630ben (tr). **27 naturepl.com:** Pete Oxford. **28 Alamy Stock Photo:** Clarence Holmes Wildlife (tr). **Dorling Kindersley:** Asia Orlando 2022. **29 Alamy Stock Photo:** Nature Picture Library / Jan Hamrsky (tl). Judy Gallagher. **30 Dreamstime.com:** Brian Lasenby (clb); Ondřej Prosický (tr). **30-31 Dorling Kindersley:** Asia Orlando 2022. **31 Alamy Stock Photo:** hemis.fr / GUIZIOU Franck (br). **naturepl.com:** Daniel Heuclin (tr). **32-33 Dorling Kindersley:** Asia Orlando 2022 (illustrations). **32 Dreamstime.com:** Narint Asawaphisith (br). **Getty Images:** Corbis Documentary / Robert Pickett. **33 Dreamstime.com:** Henrikhl (cl). **34-35 Dorling Kindersley:** Asia Orlando 2022. **34 Getty Images / iStock:** kikkerdirk. **35 Alamy Stock Photo:** Minden Pictures / Konrad Wothe (clb). **36 Alamy Stock Photo:** Minden Pictures / Donald M. Jones (br). **inaturalist.org:** By spidereyes (tl). **36-37 Dorling Kindersley:** Asia Orlando 2022. **37 Alamy Stock Photo:** Minden Pictures / Silvia Reiche (clb). **Dreamstime.com:** I Wayan Sumatika (cr). **38 Alamy Stock Photo:** Clarence Holmes Wildlife (c); Nature Picture Library / Michael Durham (cr). **38-39 Dorling Kindersley:** Asia Orlando 2022. **39 Alamy Stock Photo:** Nigel Cattlin. **naturepl.com:** Nick Upton (tl). **40-41 Dorling Kindersley:** Asia Orlando 2022. **40 Alamy Stock Photo:** Amazon-Images (r). **41 Dreamstime.com:** Moose Henderson (br). **naturepl. com:** John Cancalosi (l). **42 Shutterstock.com:** Alec Bochar Photography (tc). **42-43 Dorling Kindersley:** Asia Orlando 2022. **Getty Images:** Photodisc / Ed Reschke (t). **44 Alamy Stock Photo:** Norman Owen Tomalin (tl). **Dreamstime.com:** Derrick Neill (crb). **44-45 Dorling Kindersley:** Asia Orlando 2022 (illustrations). **45 Alamy Stock Photo:** Annelies Leeuw (cr); Minden Pictures / Norbert Wu (bl). **46-47 Alamy Stock Photo:** Pally. **47 Dorling Kindersley:** Asia Orlando 2022 (r). **48 Dorling Kindersley:** Asia Orlando 2022 (illustrations). **Dreamstime.com:** Geoffrey Kuchera (br). **49 Alamy Stock Photo:** blickwinkel / A. Hartl (crb). **Shutterstock.com:** Agnieszka Bacal. **50 Alamy Stock Photo:** S.Tuengler - inafrica.de (br).

**Dreamstime.com:** Matee Nuserm (cla). **50-51 Dorling Kindersley:** Asia Orlando 2022 (illustrations). **51 Dreamstime.com:** Orionmystery (br). **Getty Images / iStock:** FRANKHILDEBRAND (tl). **52 naturepl.com:** Ingo Arndt (cl). **52-53 Alamy Stock Photo:** Nature Picture Library / Bence Mate (t). **Dorling Kindersley:** Asia Orlando 2022 (illustrations). **54-55 Dorling Kindersley:** Asia Orlando 2022 (illustrations). **54 Alamy Stock Photo:** Minden Pictures / Michael & Patricia Fogden (crb). **55 Alamy Stock Photo:** Minden Pictures / Michael & Patricia Fogden. **56 Alamy Stock Photo:** Anthony Pierce; Anthony Pierce (bc). **57 Alamy Stock Photo:** Pally (bl). **Dorling Kindersley:** Asia Orlando 2022 (cr). **58-59 Dorling Kindersley:** Asia Orlando 2022 (illustrations). **Dreamstime.com:** Dwiputra18 (t). **60 Alamy Stock Photo:** Nature Picture Library / Anup Shah (bl). **Getty Images:** 500px / Vitor Dubinkin (cr). **60-61 Dorling Kindersley:** Asia Orlando 2022 (illustrations). **61 Alamy Stock Photo:** Svetlana Foote (cr); George Grall (bl). **Dorling Kindersley:** Asia Orlando 2022 (bc, clb). **62-63 Alamy Stock Photo:** Avalon.red / Anthony Bannister (t). **Dorling Kindersley:** Asia Orlando 2022 (illustrations). **62 Leslie Larson:** (tl). **64 naturepl.com:** Paul Hobson; Winfried Wisniewski (cra). **65 Dorling Kindersley:** Asia Orlando 2022 (r). **naturepl.com:** David Woodfall (tc). **66-67 Dorling Kindersley:** Asia Orlando 2022. **66 Alamy Stock Photo:** Organica (bl). **Science Photo Library:** Geoff Kidd (cra). **67 Dreamstime.com:** Andreistanescu (br). **68-69 Dorling Kindersley:** Asia Orlando 2022 (illustrations). **68 Alamy Stock Photo:** AfriPics.com (cla). **Getty Images / iStock:** Stramyk (b). **69 Alamy Stock Photo:** imageBROKER / Guenter Fischer (t). **70-71 Dorling Kindersley:** Asia Orlando 2022 (illustrations). **Theo Groen:** (t). **72-73 Dorling Kindersley:** Asia Orlando 2022. **72 Dreamstime.com:** Bos11 (tr); Chon Kit Leong (bc). **73 Alamy Stock Photo:** blickwinkel / F. Hecker. **Dreamstime.com:** Roman Popov (cr). **74-75 Dorling Kindersley:** Asia Orlando 2022. **74 Alamy Stock Photo:** blickwinkel / Hartl (tc). **naturepl. com:** Nature Production (clb). **75 Nature In Stock:** Thijs van den Burg (clb). **naturepl.com:** Wild Wonders of Europe / Lundgren (cr). **76-77 Dorling Kindersley:** Asia Orlando 2022 (illustrations). **Dreamstime.com:** Lori Martin (t). **77 Dreamstime.com:** Lukas Blazek (cr).

**Cover images:** *Front:* **Dreamstime.com:** Ecophoto tl; **naturepl.com:** Tim Fitzharris bl, Anup Shah br; **Shutterstock.com:** Image Source on Offset / Ken Kiefer 2 tr; *Back:* **Alamy Stock Photo:** Patrick Hudgell bl; **naturepl.com:** Franco Banfi br, SCOTLAND: The Big Picture tl, ZSSD tr.

All other images © Dorling Kindersley
For further information see: www.dkimages.com

**Josette would like to thank**
My agent, Alice Williams, for being so enthusiastic about the book from the very start and for finding it such a perfect home with DK. And the fabulously supportive and creative DK team themselves, especially editor James Mitchem and designers Charlotte Milner and Bettina Myklebust Stovne.

Asia Orlando, whose illustrations have brought our book to life and made it so much more beautiful and fun than I ever could have imagined.

My partner, Nick, for the constant help, love, and encouragement. And Peggy, my dog, who was less practically helpful but always available for snuggles. I hope neither of you ever get eaten.

**DK would like to thank**
Caroline Twomey for proofreading; Marie Lorimer for indexing; Laura Barwick for picture research; Rituraj Singh for picture library assistance; Pankaj Sharma for DTP assistance, and Alice Williams of Alice Williams Literary.

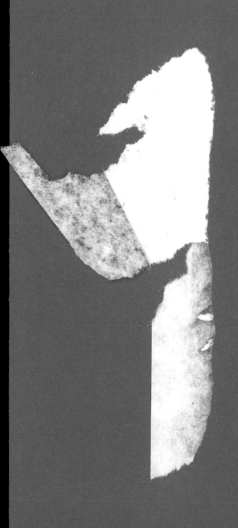